Recoveries

poems by

Peter Snow

Finishing Line Press
Georgetown, Kentucky

Recoveries

Copyright © 2021 by Peter Snow
ISBN 978-1-64662-523-9 First Edition
All rights reserved under International and Pan-American Copyright Conventions. No part of this book may be reproduced in any manner whatsoever without written permission from the publisher, except in the case of brief quotations embodied in critical articles and reviews.

This chapbook was made possible in part by donations to the ONE LAST WORD Program. ONE LAST WORD helps to bring the last works of gifted poets to the world.

Publisher: Leah Huete de Maines

Editor: Christen Kincaid

Cover Art: Vollon, Antoine, Paris Museums, Public Domain

Author Photo: Malisa Garlieb

Cover Design: Elizabeth Maines McCleavy

Order online: www.finishinglinepress.com
also available on amazon.com

Author inquiries and mail orders:
Finishing Line Press
PO Box 1626
Georgetown, Kentucky 40324
USA

with thanks to Malisa

Le coeur a ses raisons que la raison ne connaît point.
[The heart has its reasons that reason knows nothing about.]
—Blaise Pascal

I

On a terrace overlooking the valley, people holding glasses of bland wine talk to each other, unsure of names. Time has set, like aspic. Their masks are in place.

A song on the radio comes to an end and nothing has changed. There are some who watch, intense as hawks. These are the doctors. They know what is at the root of their patients' problems. They are still searching for the cure.

The beat of wings fills the mountain air. Silence reaches deep into the ears, searching for echoes. A shadow passes, and the world begins again.

II

Do we walk about foolishly, like men who have built a wall for protection and forgotten the door? With each sunrise, something, a little, seems to be gained. Something has been overcome, a spell removed. Part of a spell has been removed. The poisoned magic lingers.

War is in the distance, its thunder shaking the ground where we stand, its long fingers tracing the fault lines under our soil, cracking windowpanes and plaster, shaking pictures of calm landscapes off the walls.

One sits alone, at a distance from the rest, his chair turned away from the others. He reads a book of Japanese poetry in translation.

III *First consultation*

The Doctor's eyes swim up behind the lenses of his spectacles like curious fish in an aquarium. He is powerful and inscrutable, like a Sung emperor. The sign on his door reads 'Physician Superintendent.'

"Tell me again my dear: You can make it into a story, if you like."

She said, "One night, no words: that was the contract unspoken but understood. Even the gods cannot alter fate.

No words because we are in a hurry. So, it was supposed to happen in a pocket of time. One night; only one night, for we are impatient, and no words, because they bind and remind of the other's humanity.

And that is the true object of desire: a universe of meaning that cannot be explored in one night, even though such an exploration might require no words."

The Doctor suggests: "Perhaps it ends in a sanatorium by a lake with mountains mirrored in its surface, and two people placed carefully beside each other on the sunlit terrace. Do you think so?"

She sits with legs crossed, the upper leg kicking the air. The doctor's eyes are remote, like something glimpsed on a riverbed.

IV   *A walk in the mountains*

The patient's breath is short, his feet are blistered in the heavy boots.

Things are as they are. I climb this rugged path to the white house at the cliff top. The sound of my beating heart fills my ears, my ribs can scarcely hold it.

Don't be afraid of the mirror at the top of the stairs beyond the doorway. However ugly it looks, it's only you. The light can play tricks.

Things are as they are, the sea, the sky blue as reverence, the whiteness of the veranda wall.

Don't slip, or you drag an angel down. He will make no accusation, but he will be changed.

The air is full of the hilarity of seagulls. Where is the path? Don't look down. The light can play tricks. Things are as they are and will end as they must. Where is the path? Somehow, my feet still touch something solid.

V

In the land of the eight islands
I searched in vain for a woman,
when, beneath a Spring sky
I learned that there was
a beautiful girl;
I learned that there was
a gifted girl.

I pushed the finely carved wooden door
and it opened at my touch.
I took my beloved by the feet;
I took my beloved by the head.
I embraced my life's star.
Her arms encircled me
My arms enfolded my beloved,
like tendrils of honeysuckle
as we were united.
We slept a delicious sleep
until the cock sang in the yard.

'It is a bird on the moors,
a pheasant that sings.'

Before I could speak all
the tenderness that lay on my heart,
the day had come.
O, my beloved!

The nurses in bright uniforms with watches at the breast, catching the sunlight, bring tea on a rattling trolley, filling the cups from a steel pot catching the sunlight.

VI

At sunset, the rumble of artillery shudders the casements. The Doctor looks briefly at the window and turns back to his book. There is comfort in the sense of a culture. He believes it can help to overcome what destroys relationships between people, what is so destructive in human relations.

The fear is that for spiritual health, a further step in evolution is required. He puts the thought away and yawns.

Night falls again and the stars follow their rational courses.

She comes to see him again, her fingers touching lightly the spines of the books in his library, lips barely moving, whispering the titles.

These words touch something: what inspiration is like, what spiritual health must be like; rising to the unknown like a snail's horn stretching in ignorance towards the light.

She takes down *Discussions with the Nominalists* disturbing the dust. She reads: 'What does it matter if dry Logic has replaced Dialectics among the Seven Lively Arts? What does it matter if certainty can be found within the bounds of the question? Will those gifts turn to poison when used without care for their Divine provenance? Or can they yet bring humankind towards their own, freely found epiphanies?'

She sighs, snapping it shut with a fine spray of dust. The Doctor clears his throat.

"Tell me again about these mountains?"

"There was no disguising veil of orange light; no traffic noise. Heaven was closer, the stars nearer, taking their places as the night deepened, like a silent audience, their attention undivided, watching how we act out and improvise on their compositions. Or perhaps they were, rather, doctors, looking into us to perform their loving surgery while sleep anaesthetised us.

Certainly, something was happening that you could call theatre."

"Yes. And in the daytime?"

"The sky shone through holes in the turf: there is no name for its colour. Like peach blossom, the colour of life. The mountains bore on their shoulders heavy clouds; gravity their business. But we were on a springy raft of peat and heather, stretching across the sky, drawing from it into our limbs the equal and opposite force of levity. The bark of a fox in the night, a stag's hooves beating into the distance of the forest. I remember a wood-ants' nest, moving, rich with activity. There was the summer sun and the sound of the cold stream."

My lover has been traveling
for so long, now.
Would I, if I went, meet him
among the mountain passes,
or should I possess my soul
patiently waiting?

VII   *Confession*

Now it is the man's turn. The Doctor wipes his glasses. They need constant polishing.

"Yes. You say even the gods cannot interfere with fate. You have read your classics. But afterwards?"

"We took to our separate streets, separate lives, unconnectable dreams. From the first, she hated me for raising the question. And I have no gift for the tragic. And yet our pulses met in the mutual mistake, our masks too tightly in place. We kept finding ways back to each other."

I searched in vain for a woman.

"Later, while trying to salvage our hearts, the shape emerged from beneath the middens of contempt, the shape of what we separately longed for, somewhere else, with someone else, the form, the outline of love. The yellow oblongs of light of the windows and the thought of warmth waiting indoors, the sense of another chamber in the heart."

He turns a coin in his fingers; it catches the sunlight.

VIII   *Words of comfort*

The Doctor regards himself in the mirror, with his glasses on, and without.

"How they would characterise me matters, for that would be what they describe to the world, and I am forced to be a stickler for the truth."

Our life in this world,
what is it like?

A boat that has sailed early,
leaving no wake.

The war appears on the TV screen, full of remote, unassuageable agonies, unreachable misery, sorrow spoken in unknown tongues. The Doctor searches himself for the right, the compassionate responses. He is satisfied. The war is still far away, and his instincts are in all in place. The building shivers in sympathy as something explodes far away. He carefully knots his necktie in the shivering room.

IX   *Give me their names*

She remembers a car journey, the unfolding of well-known roads through strange landscapes, veiled in familiarity; a couple walk through a field, two horses gallop over the tussocks. Sheep are herded across a bridge; a girl walks down a village street. A man has made unexpected choices about his facial hair. Carloads of unexplored universes urge themselves forward.

She touches the brooch at her breast.

The Doctor clears his throat:

"The fibres of other lives brush the fibres of ours, and once again, the fabric is refolded."

What did we witness, after all? The trees moved in the wind, a dog barked, a horse galloped away in a field, a light came on in a distant house. What shall we tell? Allow us to speak of miracles.

The Doctor turns from her to look into the distance. What do they call the flowers that grow on the distant hillsides? And those birds with unexpected flashes of colour in the woods? Things are as they are. What are their names? And there's the animal that comes in the middle of the night, rooting in the garden. Give me their names and I shall know them.

She sits listless on a leather chair as he gazes out of the window. There is a bowl of hydroponic fruit upon his desk.

Our life in this world,
what is it like?

X   *An impossible thing*

But now it is the man's turn again. The Doctor speaks, polishing his spectacles, his eyes small and moist.

"Let us examine the facts: facts are things that can be examined. They render themselves susceptible of analysis. They speak for themselves. Good. The statue, you say, had once been painted, and two shadowy discs remained for the irises of the eyes. Then, you claim, as you looked, the eyes turned to look at you and then moved back to their original positions. I put it to you that such could not possibly happen. It must have been a delusion, a trick of the light, wishful thinking. Yet you insist."

Dust falls like spirit into matter in the sunbeams.

"Yes. I insist because I must. The impossible thing happened. It is not a failure of my cognition. Allow us to speak of miracles."

Later, the Doctor is troubled by a recollection:

Rain out of a blue sky; it can happen sometimes; or dew blown from trees? It is not impossible. I felt it today, rain out of a blue sky. The trees were blown dry long since. So, it must have been rain. Just rain out of a blue sky. Some rational explanation.

He dismisses the thought like blowing out a match. His books, his large and heavy desk, the leather upholstery; yes, he is, after all, a cultured man.

Warplanes roar overhead, and are already far away, though the air is crowded, bustling with their raging noise. He touches the knot of his tie.

XI   *The Doctor dreams again*

The Emperor stood at his window and as far as his eyes could see he created his world, his mind the essence of all outside it. The royal self he had created looked at him from the mirror and was satisfied. His peacocks and panthers strutted and prowled among his jasmine and aromatic trees; a fountain plashed in his pool of carp. But what was that bird? No one had ever seen such a creature. The Emperor saw it rise and consulted his memory. No, it was new.

He turned from the bright window to ponder in the shadows.

Suddenly he is startled awake by a noise. The scuffle of boots in the dim street in the small hours; the creak of leather greatcoats at the door; the white tiles, and dripping taps echoing in the torture room. Is that what he must fear? The shouting on the stairs of fanatics with guns?

But it was just the rattle of the tea trolley. For him, it was only tea.

XII   A dog dies

The nurses talk among themselves. A male nurse with bare, freckled forearms, unfolds a mystery of his own.

"At first we didn't believe it. Then Tom came back and said it was all true. That convinced some, those who thought Tom was a good bloke, but it wasn't good enough for me. Then two or three others burst in with the news. That changed a lot of people's minds, but I don't reckon you can be too careful. So, I held my peace and didn't say a yea or a nay.

Well, when the dog died, it convinced a lot of the others who were still swithering. A voice at the back of my mind said the dog was old, after all. It could have been natural. But I was one voice amongst many, and so I went along with it. But something is changing, all right. The war over there's just a tiny part of it."

XIII

Tea is brought in, and we all relax into quiet chatter, dropping biscuit crumbs. She accepts her medicine with a smile and will get rid of it later.

Our boat moves forward
as its rows of oars dip and rise.
Following to our captain's orders.
We navigate the rocks.

XIV   *Time becomes space*

The Doctor's journal entry:

Looking back over my life, it's like a city; I turn and walk through dark stinking alleys, and dingy side streets, loud with cursing, past the shebeens and brothels, past fights and grudging looks from dirty windows, or turn into broad avenues, full of noisy men. There are houses where women weep and children are hurt, or afraid.

There are occasional bursts of laughter. I keep walking, looking for broad boulevards of handsome buildings in the sunlight, summer parks and fountains, and happy, innocent people.

To go further, the heart needs a fifth chamber.

XV

There is a language that describes the world in the gaps between things, between breaths, between light and shadow, in words that don't always quite seem to fit. Like flashing neon reflected in a puddle, my notions come.

To be alive in a body of flesh and blood is to be swallowed by the dragon; to transform the dragon from within. And yet how we feel the skin itching beneath our dragon scales.

To know where it itches is to know what must be healed; or there can be no fifth chamber.

Perhaps I know these gestures, these attitudes, these faces after all. The masks begin to dissolve. What truly heals?

She sees him on the terrace. He has been out in the rain, but the sun is shining now. His oilskin raincoat catches the light.

He sees her in the doorway, the brooch at her breast shining. There is a rush of recognition.

XVI   *The fifth chamber*

Can something be happening without our knowing? Things are as they are, but how are they ending?

The Moon, as it traverses
and illumines the sky
is so pure, that, even veiled
by clouds, her light
is not weakened.

'Wherever two or three are gathered' comes to mind. The air is fresh on our revealed faces. Things are as they are and will end as they must. Even the gods cannot alter fate, yet we allow plenty of space for angels to pass.

What does it mean, an evolved heart?

A patient is painting a picture of the gates of Eden opening again. He whispers to himself: "A second bite of the apple."

The nurses bring biscuits and tea on a rattling trolley, pouring from a steel teapot, catching the sunlight. There is talk on the radio of a ceasefire.

The pair stand together, their shadows behind them. The Physician Superintendent watches.

"Something is moving in them that is not moving in me."

The solitary reader shuts his book.

P**eter Snow's** life was shaped by a delight in words. As a young, sickly child living outside London he listened to his father's bedside storytelling and read voraciously. Later, his love of language led him to the dramatic arts, foreign languages, and a degree in English from Edinburgh University. Peter could comfortably converse in French, Scots Gaelic, Danish, and German.

The insights of Rudolf Steiner gradually became a cornerstone of Peter's life; he worked in Camphill villages, Waldorf schools, and led Waldorf teacher trainings. His book, *A Rosslyn Treasury: Stories and Legends from Rosslyn Chapel*, grew from his related interest in the Knights Templar and alchemy.

His thirty years of teaching English and drama shaped a storyteller who could engage the hearts of young children, teens, and adults with one tale. His resonant voice, with its Scottish accent from his many years in Edinburgh, sparked magic within a listener. His book, *The Shifty Lad and the Tales He Told: Celtic Folk Stories*, is full of just such enthralling, merry mischief. Peter's artistry extended still further into music, drawing, and comics, though poetry was a life-long love.

This book may be considered his final words.

www.ingramcontent.com/pod-product-compliance
Lightning Source LLC
LaVergne TN
LVHW041525070426
835507LV00013B/1832